Artful Antics

I thought this was charming
so I bought you a copy.

Bill xxx

Artful Anticks

Artful Anticks

By

Oliver Herford

New York
The Century Co.
1901

THE DE VINNE PRESS.

Table of Contents.

The pictures in "The Point of View" are used by permission of Messrs. Harper and Brothers

Artful Anticks

The Audacious Kitten.

URRAY!" cried the kitten, "Hurray!"
　As he merrily set the sails;
"I sail o'er the ocean to-day
　　To look at the Prince of Wales!"

"O kitten! O kitten!" I cried,
　"Why tempt the angry gales?"
"I 'm going," the kitten replied,
　"To look at the Prince of Wales!

"I know what it is to get wet,
　I 've tumbled full oft into pails
And nearly been drowned—and yet
　I *must* look at the Prince of Wales!"

"O kitten!" I cried, "the Deep
  Is deeper than many pails!"
Said the kitten, "I shall not sleep
  Till I 've looked at the Prince of Wales!"

"O kitten! pause at the
    brink,
  And think of the sad sea
    tales."
"Ah, yes," said the kitten,
  "but think,
  Oh, think of the Prince
    of Wales!"

2

"But, kitten!" I cried, dismayed,
　"If you live through the angry gales
　You *know* you will be afraid
　　To look at the Prince of Wales!"

Said the kitten, "No such thing!
　Why should he make me wince?
If '*a Cat may look at a King,*'
　　A kitten may look at a Prince!"

The Artful Ant.

Once on a time an artful Ant
　　Resolved to give a ball,
For tho' in stature she was scant,
　　She was not what you 'd call
A shy or bashful little Ant.
　　(She was not shy at all.)

She sent her invitations through
　　The forest far and wide,
To all the Birds and Beasts she knew,
　　And many more beside.
("You never know what you can do,"
　　Said she, "until you 've tried.")

Five score acceptances came in
　　Faster than she could read.
Said she: "Dear me! I 'd best begin
　　To stir myself indeed!"
(A pretty pickle she was in,
　　With five-score guests to feed!)

4

The artful Ant sat up all night,
　A-thinking o'er and o'er,
How she could make from nothing, quite
　Enough to feed five-score.
(Between ourselves I think she might
　Have thought of that before.)

She thought, and thought, and thought all night,
　And all the following day,
Till suddenly she struck a bright
　Idea, which was—(but stay!
Just what it was I am not quite
　At liberty to say.)

Enough, that when the festal day
　Came round, the Ant was seen
To smile in a peculiar way,

As if — (but you may glean
From seeing tragic actors play
The kind of smile I mean.)

From here and there and everywhere
The happy creatures came,
The Fish alone could not be there.
(And they were not to blame.
" They really could not stand the air,
But thanked her just the same.")

The Lion, bowing very low,
  Said to the Ant: "I ne'er
Since Noah's Ark remember so
  Delightful an affair." ·
(A pretty compliment, although
  He really was n't there.)

They danced, and danced, and danced,
     and danced ;
  It was a jolly sight!
They pranced, and pranced, and pranced,
     and pranced,
  Till it was nearly light!
And then their thoughts to supper chanced
  To turn. (As well they might!).

Then said the Ant: "It 's only right
   That supper should begin,
And if you will be so polite,
   Pray *take each other in.*"
(The emphasis was very slight,
   But rested on "*Take in.*")

They needed not a second call,
   They took the hint. Oh, yes,
The largest guest "took in" the small,
   The small "took in" the less,
The less "took in" the least of all.
   (It was a great success!)

As for the rest— but why
   spin out
This narrative of woe ?—
The Lion took them in
   about
   As fast as they could go.
(And went home looking
   very stout,
   And walking very slow.)

And when the Ant, not long ago,
   Lost to all sense of shame,
Tried it again, I chance to know
   That not one answer came.
(Save from the Fish, who "could not go,
   But thanked her all the same.")

The GIFTED ANT.

A GIFTED ANT, who could no more
Than keep starvation from her door,
Once cast about that she might find
An occupation to her mind.

An ant with active hands and feet
Can, as a rule, make both ends meet.
Unhappily, this was not quite
The case with her of whom I
    write.

" Since I am gifted," she 'd
    explain,
" I ought to exercise
    my brain.
The only thing for
    me, it 's clear,
Is a professional
    career ! "

10

But no profession could she find,
Until one day there crossed her mind
The proverb bidding sluggards gaze
Upon the ant to learn her ways.

"The very thing!" she cried. "Hurray!
I 'll advertise without delay.
Things are come to a pretty pass,
If I can't teach a sluggard class!"

She set to work without delay,
And wrote some cards that very day;
And hung them in the grass — a plan
To catch the sluggard's eye. They ran

As follows:

SLUGGARDS who desire
An education to acquire
Will find it well to call to-day
Upon Professor Ant, B. A.
HER Sluggard Class, she begs to state,
Reopens at an early date
With several vacancies — a chance
Exceptional —

Terms — In Advance.

She placed at every turn that led
To her abode, a sign which read,
" Go to the Ant," and hung beside
Her picture, highly magnified.

Said she, " At least that cannot fail
To bring a Turtle, Sloth, or Snail,
A Dormouse, or a Boy, to learn
Their livelihood (and mine) to earn!

" I 'll teach them, first of all, to see
The joyousness of industry;
And they, to grasp my meaning more,
Shall gather in my winter store.

"The Beauty of Abstemiousness
I 'll next endeavor to impress
Upon their minds at meals. (N. B.
That is — if they should board with me.)

"Then Architecture they shall try
(My present house is far from dry)—
In short, all Honest Toil I 'll teach
(And they shall practise what I preach)."

14

Alas, for castles in the air! —
There's no delusion anywhere
Quite so delusive as, I fear,
Is a professional career.

So thought the ant last time we met.
She only has *one* sluggard yet,
Who scantly fills her larder shelf —
It is, I grieve to say, *herself!*

Sir Rat.

A Comedy.

Persons of the Drama.

MR. THOMAS CAT.   MASTER TOMMY CAT.

MRS. THOMAS CAT.   MISS FLUFFY CAT.

SIR RAT.

SCENE: *The barn. A basket in one corner.*

MASTER TOMMY (*looking out of the basket*).
How very big the world is, after all!
Compared to it our basket seems quite small,
We never dreamed, dear Fluffy, till our eyes
Were opened, that the world was such a size.
I 'd like at once to see it all.   Let 's go
And take a stroll around it.

FLUFFY.   No! No! No!
Mama expressly told us not to stray
Outside the basket while she was away.
Something might happen if we disobeyed.

TOMMY.   Oh, you 're a girl—of course you are afraid!

16

FLUFFY.   Suppose — oh, dear! — suppose we meet a Rat!

TOMMY.   Suppose we do, dear Fluffy, what of that?
   I will protect you with my strong right paw.
   The sight of me would fill a Rat with awe.

FLUFFY.   Would it?

TOMMY.   Of course it would.   I 'd like to see
   The Rat who 'd dare to trifle once with me,
   I do not think he 'd live to try it twice!

FLUFFY.   You are so brave!   It really would be nice
   To see the world —

TOMMY.   It will be grand.   Here goes!
   There, take my paw, and jump.   So, mind your toes!

(Fluffy jumps.)

Now we are off.   Tread softly, Sister dear,
If we 're not careful all the world may hear.

FLUFFY (*starting*).

   Oh, dear, what was that noise?   I wish we 'd stayed —

TOMMY (*trembling*).

   Be brave, dear Sister, — see, *I* 'm n'-n'-not a'-afraid.
   Whatever happens, do not make a row!

(*Enter* SIR RAT.)

SIR RAT.   Aha! what's this?

TOMMY.   Help! Murder! Mi-ow-*ow!*

FLUFFY.   Tommy, be calm! *Dear* Mr. Rat, good day.

SIR RAT (*jumping up and down*).
     Enough! enough! I did not come to play!

FLUFFY.   *Dear* Mr. Rat, how beautifully you
             dance.

SIR RAT.   You flatter me.

FLUFFY (*aside*).   It is my only chance.

       (*To* TOMMY.)

Run, Tommy! run! and
   bring dear Father-cat,
While I remain and flatter
   Mr. Rat.

(*Exit* TOMMY, *in haste*.)

(*To* SIR RAT.)

It 's very plain you learned that step in France.
I wish, dear Rat, you 'd teach *me* how to dance.

SIR RAT. I do not often dancing-lessons give;
But since you have n't very long to live,
And you are *so* polite, this once I 'll try.

FLUFFY. Thanks! thanks, dear Rat,— one dance before I die.

(*Polka music. Sir Rat dances and Fluffy applauds.*)

FLUFFY. Bravo! Sir Rat, I never saw before
Such perfect dancing! Won't you dance once more?

SIR RAT. Be done with folly, Kitten! Now at last
Your time has come. Reflect upon your past!

FLUFFY. It won't take long my past life to unfold!
In sooth, Sir Rat, I 'm only nine days old.

SIR RAT. Peace, Kitten! Hold thy peace!—thy time is past.
(*Springs upon her.*)

FLUFFY.   Miow! Miow!

(*Enter* MR. *and* MRS. CAT *and* TOMMY.)

MR. CAT.   Aha! Sir Rat, at last
I have thee; and this barn will soon, I trow,
Be rid of such a Ruffian Rat as thou!

(*They fight. Sir Rat falls.*)

MR. CAT (*sheathing his claws*).
'T is well I hastened; had I not, I fear
We soon had seen the last of Fluffy dear!

TOMMY.   Oh, dear, to think what might have been her fate!

FLUFFY (*aside*).   I learned that Polka step, at any rate.

MRS. CAT.   But luncheon 's waiting.   Come into the house.
Your father caught to-day a fine spring mouse.
And, children, when I tell you not to stray
From home, in future do not disobey!

CURTAIN.

✦ The End of Sir Rat ✦

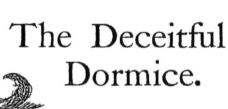

The Deceitful Dormice.

SLEEPY Dormouse who had passed
    The winter in her nest,
Hearing that spring had come at last,
    Got up at once and dressed,

And, hastening from her downy house
    To hail the new spring day,
She ran against another mouse
    That lived across the way.

The shock was such, at first the two
  Could scarcely speak for lack
Of breath.   Then each cried, " Oh, it 's *you!*
  Why, when did you get back?"

" I 've only just return'd, my dear,"
  The sleepy Dormouse said,
" From Florida — the winters here,
  You know, affect my head."

" Have you, indeed?" exclaimed her friend.
  " I 'm glad to see you home.
I, too, have just returned — I spend
  My winters down in Rome."

With many pawshakes then, at last
  They parted — each to say,
" I wonder where that creature passed
  The winter — anyway!"

23

Nature and Art.

SAID a lady who wore a
  swell cape,
As she viewed a Rhinoc-
  eros, agape,
   "To think in this age
   A Beast in a cage
Is permitted our fashions
  to ape!"

Thought the Beast in the
  cage, "I declare,
One would think that these
  Ladies so fair
   Who come to the Zoo
   Have nothing to do
But copy the things that
  I wear!"

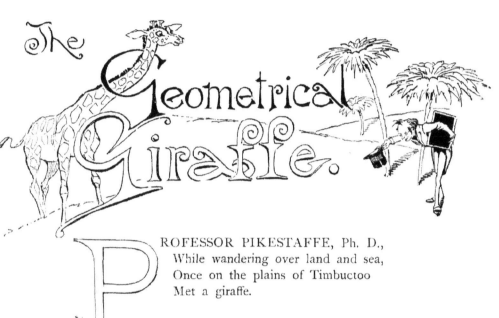

The Geometrical Giraffe.

ROFESSOR PIKESTAFFE, Ph. D.,
While wandering over land and sea,
Once on the plains of Timbuctoo
Met a giraffe.

"Why, how d' ye do!"
Exclaimed the amiable Pikestaffe.
"I 'm really charmed, my dear Giraffe!
I 've thought so much of you of late,
Our meeting seems a stroke of Fate
Particularly fortunate.
I long have had upon my mind
Something concerning you; be kind
Enough to seat yourself, and pray
Excuse, if what I have to say
Seems personal!"

"My dear Pikestaffe,
I shall be charmed," said the Giraffe,
"To hear whatever you may say.
    You are too kind; go on, I pray."

"Well, then," said Pikestaffe, "to resume,
    You are aware, sir, I presume,
    That though with your long neck at ease
    You crop the leaves upon the trees,
    Your legs are quite *too* long, and make
    It difficult for you to slake
    Your thirst—in other words, you 've found
    Your neck too short to reach the ground.
    Indeed, I 've often wept to think
    How hard it is for you to drink.

" To right a wrong we must, of course,
First try to ascertain the source ;
And in this case we find the cause
In certain geometric laws,
Which I will quickly demonstrate
(How lucky that I brought my slate !).

" Well, to begin, let line A B

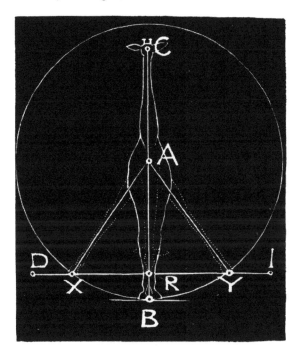

Be your front legs; then line A C
(A shorter line) your neck shall be.
Measured, 't will only reach so far,
When bent down toward the ground, as R.

27

Then R's your head stretched down, and shows
How far the ground lies from your nose—
Though if the ground lay not at B,
But R, you 'd reach it easily.
Suppose it then at R to lie,
And draw for ground line D R I.
Your head then touches ground at R —
But now your feet go down too far!

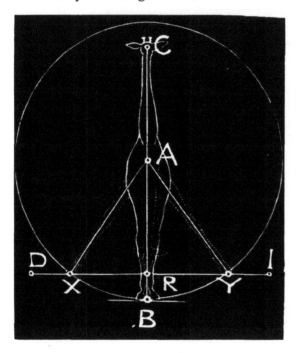

My compasses then I will lay
On A and B, and make round A
A circle crossing line D I
At two points. Mark them X and Y;

Then draw from X and Y to A
Two lines; then it is safe to say
That line A X and line A Y
Equal A B, *being radii*
Of the same circle, as you see
(According to geometry).
But since at first we did agree
A B your length of leg should be,
These, being equal to A Б,
Are just the same as legs, you see.
So now on legs A X, A Y.
You stand upon
  the ground
  D I,
And drink your
  fill; for, as I
  said,
D I is touched
  by R, your head.

Thus we have proved —"

*   *   *   *   *

What happened here
Professor Pikestaffe has no clear
Impression, but the little row
Of stars above will serve to show
What madly reeled before his eyes,
As he went whirling to the skies.
Below he heard a mocking laugh,
That seemed to come from the Giraffe :
" Go up! go up! You 've proved
    enough ;
You 've proved geometry is stuff!
You 've proved, till I am well nigh
    dead,
And feel a thumping in my head,
That I must spread my feet apart
To take a drink — why, bless
    your heart !

I knew that long ere you were born.
I laugh geometry to scorn."

      *   *   *   *   *

Professor Pikestaffe, Ph. D.,
They say, has dropped geometry—
It seems he dropped his slate as well,
Which lies exactly where it fell
(Also the diagram he drew)
Upon the plains of Timbuctoo.

The Early Owl

AN Owl once lived in a hollow tree,
And he was as wise as wise could be.
The branch of Learning *he* did n't know
Could scarce on the tree of knowledge grow.
He knew the tree from branch to root,
And an Owl like that can afford to hoot.

And he hooted — until, alas! one day
He chanced to hear, in a casual way,
An insignificant little bird
Make use of a term he had never heard.
He was flying to bed in the dawning light
When he heard her singing with all her might,
" Hurray! hurray for the early worm!"

"Dear me!" said the Owl, "what a singular term!
I would look it up if it were n't so late;
  I must rise at *dusk* to investigate.
Early to bed and early to rise
  Makes an Owl healthy and stealthy and wise!"

So he slept like an honest Owl all day,
  And rose in the early twilight gray,
And went to work in the dusky light
  To look for the early worm all night.

He searched the country for miles around,
  But the early worm was not to be found.
So he went to bed in the dawning light,
  And looked for the " worm" again next night.

And again and again, and again and again
  He sought and he sought, but all in vain,
Till he must have looked for a year and a day
  For the early worm, in the twilight gray.

At last in despair he gave up the search,
  And was heard to remark, as he sat on his perch
By the side of his nest in the hollow tree,
" The thing is as plain as night to me —
Nothing can shake my conviction firm,
  There 's no such thing as the early worm."

A Dark Career

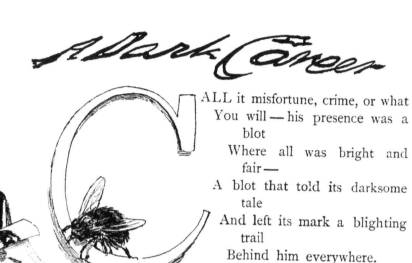

CALL it misfortune, crime, or what
  You will — his presence was a
     blot
    Where all was bright and
      fair —
A blot that told its darksome
     tale
And left its mark a blighting
     trail
    Behind him everywhere.

   .   .   .   .   .   .

He stood by the Atlantic's
    shore,
  And crossed the azure
      main,
    And even the sea, so blue
      before,
      About his wake grew
        dark and bore
        The semblance of a
          stain.

On English soil he scarcely more
  Than paused his breath to gain;
But on that fair historic shore
There seemed to gather, as before,
  A darkness in his train.

Through sunny France, across the line
To Germany, and up the Rhine
  To Switzerland he came;
Then o'er the snowy Alpine height,
To leave a stain as black as night
  On Italy's fair name.

From Italy he crossed the blue,
And hurried on as if he knew
  His journey's end he neared.
On Darkest Africa he threw
A shade of even darker hue,
  Till in the sands of Timbuctoo
  His record disappeared.

    .   .   .   .   .

Only an inkstand's overflow,
O Bumblebee! remains to show
    The source of your mishap;
But though you 've flown my
  ken beyond,
The foot-notes of your *tour
  du monde*
    Still decorate my
      map.

I.

FROM MR. RUFUS FOX TO MISS BLANCHE GOOSE.

THE FERNWOODS, Friday.

Dear Miss Goose:
Accept apologies profuse,
For the abrupt and hasty way,
In which I left you yesterday.
I don't know how I came to be
So very rude, but then you see,
I *was* just offering my arm,

37

When stupid Rover from the farm,
Appeared so suddenly, and so —
Well, two is company, you know,
While three —! Besides, 't was getting late,
So I decided not to wait.
Yet, after all, another day
Will do as well. What do you say?
Can you contrive to dine with me
To-morrow afternoon at three?
Pray do, and by the hollyhocks
Meet yours, sincerely,   RUFUS FOX.

II.

FROM MISS BLANCHE GOOSE
TO MR. FOX.

THE FARMYARD, Friday afternoon.
Dear Mr. Fox, it seems so *soon*,
You almost take my breath away!
To-morrow?   Three? — what *shall* I say?
Nothing could charm me more —
    but, no —
Alas! I fear I cannot go.
Don't think that I *resent*,
    I pray,
Your hastiness of yester-
    day.

It is not that. But if I went,
Without my dear Mama's consent,
And she should somehow chance to hear,
She would be *dreadfully* severe;
And so, oh, dear! it is no use!
　　Believe me,
　　　　Sadly yours, BLANCHE GOOSE.

P. S.— On second thoughts, dear Fox,
I 'll meet you by the hollyhocks,
For if Mama but knew how *kind*
You are, I 'm sure she would not mind,
To-morrow, then—we 'll meet at *three;*
Don't fail to be there. Yours, B. G.

III.

FROM MR. RUFUS FOX TO HIS COUSIN REYNARD.

FRIDAY.
Dear Cousin, just a line
To ask if you will come to dine
(Informally, you know) with me
To-morrow afternoon at three.
Now don't refuse, whate'er
　　you do,
I have a treat in store for
　　you:
A charming goose (and
　　geese, you know,
Do not on all the bushes
　　grow!)

A dream of tenderness in white,
A case of "hunger at first sight."
I know, old boy, you 'll not be deaf
To *this* inducement.

Yours,   R. F.

P. S.—Miss Goose agrees to be
Beside the hollyhocks at three!

IV.

EXTRACT FROM THE DIARY OF ROVER,
THE DOG.

SATURDAY NIGHT.

Well, I must say,
I quite renewed my youth to-day!
How lucky that I chanced to go,
Just when I did, beside that row
Of hollyhocks beyond the gate!
Lucky for *her* at any rate;
For suddenly I heard Miss Goose
Struggling and crying, "Let me loose!"
And, from behind the hollyhocks,
Who should jump out but Mr. Fox!
(The very same one, by the way,
I *almost* caught the other day.)
Soon as I nabbed him, in his fright,
He dropped Miss Goose and took to flight

Then after him like mad I flew,
But—what could poor old Rover do?
I am not what I used to be,
So I let go, and ran to see
At once how poor Miss Goose had fared,
And found her much less hurt than scared
From having come so near the noose:—
A sadder and a wiser goose.

V.

NOTE FROM MR. RUFUS FOX TO HIS
COUSIN REYNARD.

DEAR COUSIN:
            This is just to say
Why dinner was postponed to-day,—
The goose had failed us, that was all;
Excuse, I beg, this hurried scrawl.
Will write to-morrow to explain—

Just now my paw is in such pain
That when I try to write it shocks
My nerves.

        Yours truly,   Rufus Fox.

P. S.— I 'd thank you if you sent
A bottle of that liniment
You spoke of several days ago—
The kind for " dog-bites," don't you know.

ONCE a naughty fay
  Chanced to sprain her wing;
"At her tricks," they say —
  "Naughty little thing!"

Said the little fay
  As she lay in pain,
"No more tricks I'll play
  When I'm well again."

43

Time heals everything.
　Can this be our fay,
She who sprained her wing
　Just the other day?

Can she be this fair
　Thrifty little thing,
Sewing up a tear
　In a beetle's wing?

Yes,—alas! but oh,
　Not a thrifty elf;
Of course she has to sew
　What she tore herself!

The Miller's Quest

(A Floury Tale.)

THE Princess' hair hath golden sheen,
    And her cheek is lily-pale;
But none may look in her eyes, I ween
    And live to tell the tale.

From out the south, and eke the north,
    And from the east and west,
Full many a gallant knight rides forth
    Upon the fatal quest.

For a cruel spell on the Princess lies
    No mortal can undo
Till one shall look into her eyes
    And tell their color true.

46

And some of them swear her eyes are green,
   And some that they are black,
And many a knight rides forth, I ween,
   But never a one rides back.

For a cruel spell on
   the Princess lies,
  And whoso will may try
His fate, and look into her
   eyes;
  But whoso quails must die.

The miller's son is a dusty youth,
   And dusty curls hath he.
Quoth he, "I 'll go myself, forsooth,
   And set this Princess free."

47

The miller's son he hath no spear
  Nor sword nor coat-of-mail,
But an honest heart that knows not fear —
  Heaven grant he may not fail!

The miller's son at the portal knocks,
  At the Princess' feet he bends,
And he tosses aside his floury locks
  And a floury cloud ascends.

The Princess' face in a mist of white
  Is veiled as with a veil,
Her eyes are dimmed of their deadly
      light,
    And the miller doth not quail.

The Princess' hair hath golden sheen,
Her cheek is red, red rose,
And her eyes?
       .   .   .

              Go ask the Prince—
                   I mean
The miller's son—he knows.

Nell's Fairy-tal

THE fairy tale was ended, the wicked
    Queen had fled;
The Prince had saved the Princess
    and cut off the monster's head;
The people all were joyful, and the
    Princess and the Prince
Were married and—so ran the tale
    —"lived happy ever since."
Nell closed the book of fairy tales
    and mused: "I wonder why
There are no fairies nowadays? I
    only wish that I

Could be a fairy princess like the Princess Goldenhair."
Here Nell dropped off to sleep, and then she started in her chair,
When, of its own accord, the book popped open, and behold!
Out crept a wee elf-princess all arrayed in cloth of gold;
She sighed a little tired sigh and then Nell heard her say,
In a tiny tired little voice, that sounded far away:
" Oh, dear! how very nice it is for once to get outside.
You 've no idea how flat it is, my dear, until you 've tried,
To be shut up in a story-book with Dragons, Queens, and Kings,
And always have to do and say the same old, senseless things;
You think it would be very fine, but really it 's no joke!
I 'd rather be a girl, like *you!*—"

Then little Nell awoke,
" Poor Princess Goldenhair," said she,—" unhappy little elf,
I 'm rather glad, upon the whole, that I am just myself!"

The Unfortunate Giraffe.

THERE was once a Giraffe who said, " What
    Do I want with my tea strong or
      hot ?
      For my throat 's such a length,
      The tea loses its strength,
  And is cold ere it reaches the
      spot."

Stockings or Scales.

IF I were asked of all things what I most would like to be,
I 'd choose to be a mermaid and live below the sea.
How nice, instead of walking, to swim around like little whales,
And to wear, instead of stockings, many shiny pairs of scales,
Which don't need changing every time that nurse says they are wet.
And then to have no shoes that always come untied!—and yet—

And yet, although it must be nice to swim around in scales,
To attend a school of porpoises and play at tag with whales,
To be on friendly speaking terms with jellyfish and eels,
And never to be sent to bed or told I 'm late for meals;
Still, when I think of Christmas Eve my resolution fails,
How could I hang my stockings up if I had only scales?

A Riddle.

HEY were three robbers; aye,
    And they robbed a red, red rose;
And they came from out the sky,
    And they went where no man knows.

One came when the day was young,
    And rent the curtain gray
Of mist that round her hung,
    And he stole her pearls away;

One came when the day was old,
    And a sable coat he wore,
And a belt of dusty gold,
    And he robbed her treasure-store.

54

One came when the day was dead,
  And no man saw him pass;
And he caught her petals red
  And threw them upon the grass.

Three robbers bold were they,
  And they robbed a red, red rose;
And they came and went away,
  And whither —

              no man knows.

Good-bye.

A WOODLAND EPISODE

PERSONS OF THE DRAMA: Miss Bird, and Mrs. Chipmunk.

Scene: The woods.   *Time:* Last November.

Miss Bird.—Why, Mrs. Chipmunk! how do you do?

Mrs. Chipmunk.— I 'm quite well, thanks, Miss Bird; and you?

Miss B.— I 'm sorry to say my health is poor,
   So my doctor has ordered a southern tour.
   Could n't you manage to come along?
   It would do you good —

Mrs. C.—   Yes, I 'm far from strong,
   And it 's just what I 'd most like to do
   If I 'd only a pair of wings —

Miss B.—   Pooh! Pooh!
   There are trains for people who cannot fly.

Mrs. C.—Yes, but the fares are so dreadfully high!
   So really I must n't think of that—

Miss B.—If only you 'd wings like your cousin Bat.

Mrs. C.—*If only!* but then I have n't, you see.
   Besides, I 've rented a hole in a tree,

56

On the first-floor branch just four trees west
Of the oak where you built your last year's nest.

MISS B.—A charming neighborhood! just the thing
For a winter home —

MRS. C.—   Well, I hope, next spring,
When you 're here again, you will try to call.

MISS B.—You are very kind —

MRS. C.—   Oh, not at all!

MISS B.— Good-by, Mrs. Chipmunk.

MRS. C.—   Oh, *must* you fly?
Then, a pleasant journey!

MISS B.—   Good-by!

MRS. C.—   *Good*-by!

The Professor and the White Violet

THE PROFESSOR.

TELL me, little violet white,
If you will be so polite,
Tell me how it came that you
Lost your pretty purple hue?
Were you blanched with sudden
fears?
Were you bleached with fairies'
tears?
Or was Dame Nature out of
blue,
Violet, when she came
to you?

THE. VIOLET.

Tell me, silly mortal, first,
Ere I satisfy your thirst
For the truth concerning me —
Why you are not like a tree?
Tell me why you move around,
Trying different kinds of ground,
With your funny legs and boots
In the place of proper roots?

Tell me, mortal, why your head,
Where green branches ought to spread,
Is as shiny smooth as glass,
With just a fringe of frosty grass?
Tell me — Why, he 's gone away!
Wonder why he would n't stay?
Can he be — well, I declare! —
Sensitive about his hair?

The First Rose of Summer

" Oh, dear! is summer over? "
  I heard a rosebud moan,
When first her eyes she opened,
  And found she was alone.

" Oh, why did summer leave me,
  Little me, belated?
Where are the other roses?
  I think they *might* have waited! "

Soon the little rosebud
  Saw to her surprise
Other roses opening,
  So she dried her eyes.

60

Then I heard her laughing
Gaily in the sun,
" I thought the summer over;
Why, it 's only just begun!"

The Elf & the Dormouse

Under a toadstool
  Crept a wee Elf,
Out of the rain
  To shelter himself.

Under the toadstool,
  Sound asleep,
Sat a big Dormouse
  All in a heap.

Trembled the wee Elf,
  Frightened, and yet
Fearing to fly away
  Lest he get wet.

To the next shelter —
  Maybe a mile!
Sudden the wee Elf
  Smiled a wee smile,

62

Tugged till the toadstool
  Toppled in two.
Holding it over him
  Gaily he flew.

Soon he was safe home
  Dry as could be.
Soon woke the Dormouse —
  " Good gracious me!

Where is my toadstool ? "
  Loud he lamented.
— And that 's how umbrellas,
  First were invented.

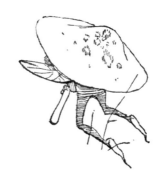

The Crocodile

CROCODILE once dropped a line
To a Fox to invite him to
dine;
But the Fox wrote to say
He was dining, that day,
With a Bird friend, and begged
to decline.

64

She sent off at once to a Goat.
" Pray don't disappoint me," she wrote ;
But he answered too late,
He 'd forgotten the date,
Having thoughtlessly eaten her note.

The Crocodile thought him ill-bred,
And invited two Rabbits instead;
　　But the Rabbits replied,
　　They were hopelessly tied
By a previous engagement, and fled.

Then she wrote in despair to some Eels,
And begged them to " drop in " to meals;
    But the Eels left their cards
     With their coldest regards,
And took to what went for their heels.

Cried the Crocodile then, in disgust,
" My motives they seem to mistrust.
        Their suspicions are base,
        Since they don't know their place,—
I suppose if I *must* starve, I *must!*"

The Forgetful Forgetmenot.

THE PROFESSOR.

RAY tell me, sweet Forget-me-not,
Oh, kindly tell me where you got
Your curious name?
I 'm most desirous to be told
The legend or romance of old
From whence it came.

FORGET-ME-NOT.

Indeed, good sir, it seems to me,
If you have books on Botany
Upon your shelf,
You 'd better far consult those books — ·
He learns a thing the best who looks
It up himself.

69

THE PROFESSOR.

> I 've works on Botany a few,
> But though I 've searched them through and through,
>> Never a word
> Can I discover in the same
> About your interesting name.

FORGET-ME-NOT.

> Why, how absurd!

THE PROFESSOR.

> Quite so! And now what can I do?
> I shall be most obliged if you
>> Will make it plain.

FORGET-ME-NOT.

> Another time. One moment
>> more,
> And you 'll be drenched!
>> It 's going to
>>> pour:
>> I felt just now
>>> no less than
>>> four
>> Big drops of
>>> rain.
> [*Exit* PROFESSOR.]

70

FORGET-ME-NOT.

> (*Aside*) Indeed, I 'd tell him if I knew ;
> But it would never, never do
>   If I explained
> That, long ago, I quite forgot
> Why I was called Forget-me-not
>   (It 's well it rained) !

The Birds' Farewell.

—

My Dear Little Maid:

We must bid you good-by,
For November is here, and it's time we should fly
To the South, where we have an engagement to sing,
But, remember this, dear, we'll return in the spring.
And if, while abroad, we hear anything new,
We'll learn it, and sing it next summer to you
In the same little tree on the lawn, if you'll let us.
So, good-by, little maiden! Please do not forget us.
We're sorry to leave you — too sorry for words,
And we'll always remain,

Yours sincerely, "The Birds."

P. S.—Please don't mind if this letter sounds flat,
And present our respectful regards to your cat.

The Spider's Tale.

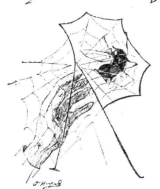

The Poet offereth
to deliver a Fly
from the
Spider's web.

" REALLY, Fly, you ought to know
Better, surely, than to go
Into Mr. Spider's net.
Luckily *I'm* here to set
You free"; but ere I could have stirred,
Mr. Spider's voice I heard
Crying in an angry tone:
" Better let my lunch alone!

Even Spiders'
rights must
be respected.

" One would think, for all *you* care,
Spiders could subsist on air.
Listen to this tale and see
If you don't agree with me!"

    .   .   .   .   .

I sat down without a word,
Following is the tale I heard:

73

THE TALE.

The Spider
spinneth a yarn
to instruct the
Poet
and divert him
that he may forget
about the Fly.

A Prince who sought
His lost Bride, caught
In the toils of a witch,— woe betide her! —
When riding one night
Through a forest, caught sight
  Of a Spi in the web of a Flyder.

74

(As perhaps you surmise,
I have tried to disguise,
   The names, with the best of intention:
For I make it my plan,
Whenever I can,
   To avoid any personal mention.)

Said the Prince to the Spi,
"Supposing that I
   Should deliver you out of this hatefulness,
Will you pay me in kind,
And help me to find
   My Bride? — Can I count on your grate-
     fulness?"

Said the Spi, "Without doubt,
If you *will* let me out
   From the web of the terrible Flyder,
By all means — oh, yes!
You shall find your Princess,
   For I will myself be your guider!"

The Flyder
does not see it in
the same light as
the Prince

One jerk! He was free,
And his buzzing and glee
     Drove the Prince to the verge of distraction.
The Flyder, meanwhile,
Wore a cynical smile,
     And a look of — well — *not* satisfaction.

The Prince paid no heed,
But mounted his steed,
     And started the Princess to find.
The Spi led the way,
But little dreamed they
     That the Flyder had mounted behind!

He found her, it 's true,
And the wicked witch, too,
     Who fled when he up and defied her;
But while being wed,
Hanging over her head,
     The Princess caught sight of the Flyder!

Showing the terri-
ble consequences
of meddling
with the domestic
affairs of a Flyder

At the terrible sight,
Her reason took flight,
     Till she was completely bereft of it,
When she drained a tureen
Full of cold Paris green,
     And the Prince swallowed all that was
          left of it!

Setting forth how
a Poet and a Fly
were both taken
in by a
Spider's yarn,
and how that a
diverting tale may
speed a good
dinner.

Listening to the Spider, I
Quite forgot poor Mr. Fly
And his pitiable plight
Till the tale was finished quite,
Then, alas! too late I knew,
Mr. Fly was finished, too.

Highly Connected.

" I 'm a very little cat,
I know, and thin at that;
But cast your eye upon
this poster fine —
The big chap on that ball,
He 's just a King, that 's
all —
And, by the way, a rela-
tive of mine ! "

The Miser Elf.

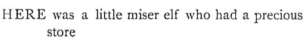

HERE was a little miser elf who had a precious
    store
    Of silver motes from moonbeams and priceless
        grains of ore,
      And shiny dust of marigold, and glittering
        jeweled eyes
        Of burnished stars and spangles from the
           wings of butterflies,
And bales of wondrous gossamer and green-gold beetles' wings,
And many other marvelous and rare and costly things.
But, alas! with all his golden dust and jewels rich and rare,
This little elf was never free from misery and care.

The wealth that might have conjured up all good things at his beck
Was just a golden millstone that hung around his neck.
He never had one moment's peace, his treasure out of sight,
Though he buried it for safety in a different place each night;
Each night the thought of robbers made him close his eyes in vain,
And just as soon as it was light he 'd dig it up again.

One night (it was a woodland place in which he chanced to bide) -
As usual he sought a place in which his gold to hide.
He had not long been seeking before he chanced to see
A thing he 'd never seen before — a curious kind of tree:

The stem was smooth and
straight, and on the top
there grew a sort
Of dome or hat—let 's call
it an umbrella-tree, for short.
"The very place ! " ex-
claimed the elf. "So
strange a tree, 't is clear,
Is just the thing to mark the
spot. I 'll hide my treasure
here."

No sooner said than done ;
and then, his treasure
buried deep,
Upon a bed of moss near by
he laid him down to sleep.
For once the elf enjoyed a
night from dreams and
terrors free ;
And, waking, sought
with bounding
step his tall um-
brella-tree.

"Ah, here it is!" he cried; and sure enough, before his sight
It stood. "But what is this?" Another like it to the right!
"Which can it be?" He rubbed his chin. "What underneath
  the sun
Has happened? Why, I could have sworn last night there was
  but one.
Which can it be that marks the spot in which my treasure lies?"
And looking round, another tree of the same shape and size,
Another and another still met his astonished eyes.

Then the dreadful truth burst on him, and he stood transfixed with
  fright
In a forest of umbrella-trees all grown up in a night.

  .   .   .   .

When walking in the autumn woods, dear reader, and you pass
A toadstool lying on its side among the leaves and grass,
Think of the little miser elf, for 't is a sign that he
Still digs for his lost treasure underneath the umbrella-tree.

The Point of View.

O N the top of the world, where
there 's lots of snow,
As all the geographies say,
A small Eskimo, just to make
the time go,
Was building a Snow Man
one day.

Now it happened by chance
that two Polar Bears
Came strolling along that way:
" Perhaps it is none of our affairs,
But what are you making ? " said they.

" A Snow Man, of course," said the Eskimo;
The Bears gave a comical stare ;

84

Said they, " If you *must* make a person of snow,
  Why on earth don't you make a Snow Bear?"

He sat himself down for a moment to think
  Of some suitable sort of reply,
When a Penguin, two Foxes, a Seal, and a Mink,
  And a Walrus came wandering by.

They stopped just a casual look to take,
  A casual word to say,
And each had a trifling suggestion to make
  In a patronizing way.

The Walrus said, " Really, it is n't half bad,
  And shows lots of promise, you know;
Yet I think, for my part, though perhaps it 's a fad,
  A Snow Walrus were more apropos."

The Foxes, the Seal, and the Mink were afraid
  They knew little of art, so they said,
But they thought he would show better taste if he made
  A Fox, Seal, or Mink in its stead.

The Penguin said nothing, nor listened, but when
   They 'd finished, he ventured to say,
" It dòes n't look *much* like a Penguin, but then
   Perhaps when completed, it may."

They turned then to go; but the Eskimo —
   Alas! he was seen no more;
The heat of his anger and shame and chagrin
Had melted the snow where the crust was thin,
   And he 'd sunk, so to speak, through the floor.

Heroes.

I BUILT a castle on the shore,
And left to guard it three or four
Lead soldiers of the bravest sort,
And ordered them to hold the fort
Till I should come once more.

But when I came again next day,
I found the sea had washed away
My castle built upon the sand.
Alas! the gallant little band
Of soldiers, where were they?

Buried in sand, erect, and square,
They held the fort with martial air;
And when I 'd said a little speech,
I dug them out and made them each
A general then and there.

Belated Violet

ERY dark the autumn sky,
  Dark the clouds that hurried by;
Very rough the autumn breeze
  Shouting rudely to the trees.

Listening, frightened, pale, and cold,
  Through the withered leaves and mold
Peer'd a violet all in dread—
  " Where, oh, where is spring? " she said.

Sighed the trees, " Poor little thing!
  She may call in vain for spring."
And the grasses whispered low,
  " We must never let her know."

89

" What 's this whispering ? " roared the breeze,
   " Hush! a violet! " sobbed the trees,
" Thinks it 's spring — poor child, we fear
    She will die if she should hear!"

Softly stole the wind away,
   Tenderly he murmured, "Stay!"
To a late thrush on the wing,
   " Stay with her one day and sing!"

Sang the thrush so sweet and clear
   That the sun came out to hear,
And, in answer to her song,
   Beamed on violet all day long.

And the last leaves here and there
  Fluttered with a spring-like air,
Then the violet raised her head —
  "Spring has come at last!" she said.

Happy dreams had violet
  All that night — but happier yet,
When the dawn came dark with snow,
  Violet never woke to know.

The Parrot and the Cuckoo.
A Tragedy.

SCENE: *The vicinity of the Cuckoo Clock.   Cuckoo discovered in the act of telling three o'clock.   Parrot watching from a perch near by.*

CUCKOO: Cuckoo! Cuckoo! Cuckoo!

PARROT: Hark, there she goes!
      To hear her any parrot would suppose
      She owned the earth, conceited little thing,
      She really seems to fancy she can sing,
      Yet, though you 'll scarce believe, that little bird
      Rules the whole blessed household with a word.
      She only has to call "Cuckoo!" and lo!

The family at once to luncheon go.
When she screams "Cuckoo!" twice it is the rule
For all the kids to hurry back to school—
And when *six* times they know it is a sign
That Cuckoo thinks it's time for them to dine.
And so it goes through all the livelong day,
She tells them what to do and they obey.
But as for me, they treat me like a doll
And mimic me and call me "Pretty Poll,"
And ask me several million times a day,
"Does Polly want a cracker?"—by the way,
I've yet to see that cracker—oh, sometimes
I gnash my beak, or mutter nursery rhymes
Or anything! for fear I should let slip
The wicked words they taught me on the ship,
Those naughty sailors, when long, long ago
They brought me from the land where spices grow

And palm-trees wave, and Cuckoos do
   not rule
And tell folks when to bed and when
   to school
And when to go to dinner.
               Never mind!
My time will come. As that vain bird
   will find
Unto her sorrow. Yes, the die is
   cast!
Next time the Cuckoo squawks will be
   her last.

Next time she tries —

CUCKOO (*striking four o'clock*): Cuckoo! Cuckoo! Cuckoo!

PARROT: Come, now, have done! we 've heard enough from you!
      Prepare to die! your little reign is o'er,
      Over this house you 'll tyrannize no more!
      What! won't you come? then I 'll soon show you how!
      There! stop that racket; heavens, what a row!

94

(Smashes the Cuckoo to bits, causing the machinery to run down.)

Help, stop it, some one!

(It stops.)

Well, upon my word,
You're tough for such a very little bird,
I thought you'd never die! and now, my dear,
The family will very soon be here,
And when they see how little's left of you
They'll be so glad they won't know what to do—
To think the Cuckoo's killed and they are free
To work or play or sleep or take their tea
Just when they please —and, best of all, how jolly
To feel they owe it all to "Pretty Polly"!

(Curtain.)

The Elf and the Bee.

" Oh, Bumblebee!
    Bumblebee!
    Don't fly so near!
Or you will tumble me
    Over, I fear !"

   " Oh, funny Elf!
     Funny Elf!
    Don't be alarmed!
I 'm looking for honey, Elf.
    You sha'n't be harmed."

     " Then tarry,
      Oh, tarry, Bee !
     Fill up your
       sack ;
     And carry,
      oh, carry me
    Home on your back !"

96

A Fable.

IT was a hungry pussy cat
 Upon Thanksgiving morn,
And she watched a thankful little mouse
 That ate an ear of corn.

"If I ate that thankful little mouse,
 How thankful he should be,
When he has made a meal himself,
 To make a meal for me!

"Then, with his thanks for having fed
 And his thanks for feeding me—
With all *his* thankfulness inside—
 How thankful *I* shall be!"

Thus mused the hungry pussy cat
 Upon Thanksgiving Day.
But the little mouse had overheard,
 And declined (with thanks) to stay.

The Fairies' Concert.

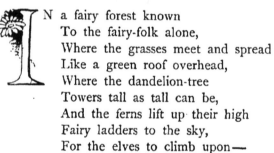

IN a fairy forest known
To the fairy-folk alone,
Where the grasses meet and spread
Like a green roof overhead,
Where the dandelion-tree
Towers tall as tall can be,
And the ferns lift up their high
Fairy ladders to the sky,
For the elves to climb upon —
Here are merry goings-on.

From the forest far and near
All the fairy-folk are here,
For to-day there is to be
Music 'neath the daisy-tree.

And the creatures of the wood,
One and all, have been so good
And obliging as to say,
They will gladly come and play
For the elves a serenade,
In the fairy forest glade.
All the little birds have come;
And the bumblebees that hum;
And the gnats that twang the lute;
And the frogs that play the flute;
And the kind of frog whose toots
Seem to come from out his boots;
And the great big green and yellow
Frog that plays upon the 'cello;
And the katydid, in green,
Who is oftener heard than seen;
With the little ladybird
Who is oftener seen than heard;
And the cricket, never still
With his lively legs and trill.
And, in short, each forest thing
That can hum, or buzz, or sing,
Each and all have come to play
For the little elves to-day.

Now the crawfish takes the stand
To conduct the fairy band.
First there is a moment's pause,
Then the leader lifts his claws,
Waves his wand, and—one, two, three!
All at once, from gnat and bee,
Frog, and katydid, and bird

99

Such a melody is heard
That the elves and fairies wee,
Clapping little hands with glee,
Make their mushroom seat to sway
In a very risky way.
And the creatures in delight
Play away with all their might,
Feeling very justly proud
That the elves applaud so loud.

Now the sun is getting low,
And the elves to bed must go
Ere the sleepy flowers close
In whose petals they repose;
For if they were late they might
Have to stay outside all night.
So the last good-byes are said;
Every one goes home to bed;
And the creatures as they fly
Play a fairy lullaby,
Growing faint and fainter still,
Fainter and more faint, until
All is silent—and the shade
Creeps upon the fairy glade.

Lightning Source UK Ltd.
Milton Keynes UK
UKHW020631150221
378806UK00008B/625